Take The Fear Out Of Cables

Leisure Arts, Inc.
Maumelle, Arkansas

EDITORIAL STAFF

Vice President of Editorial: Susan White Sullivan
Creative Art Director: Katherine Laughlin
Publications Director: Leah Lamperiz
Technical Writer/Editor: Sarah J. Green
Associate Technical Editors: Linda A. Daley, Cathy Hardy, and Lois J. Long
Editorial Writers: Susan Frantz Wiles and Susan McManus Johnson
Art Category Manager: Lora Puls
Graphic Artists: Jessica Bramlett and Becca Snider Tally
Prepress Technician: Stephanie Johnson
Contributing Photographers: Jason Masters and Ken West
Contributing Photo Stylist: Angela Alexander

BUSINESS STAFF

President and Chief Executive Officer: Rick Barton
Senior Vice President of Operations: Jim Dittrich
Vice President of Finance: Fred F. Pruss
Vice President of Sales-Retail Books: Martha Adams
Vice President of Mass Market: Bob Bewighouse
Vice President of Technology and Planning: Laticia Mull Dittrich
Controller: Tiffany P. Childers
Information Technology Director: Brian Roden
Director of E-Commerce: Mark Hawkins
Manager of E-Commerce: Robert Young
Retail Customer Service Manager: Stan Raynor

Library of Congress Control Number: 2013948965

ISBN-13: 978-1-60900-413-2

20

36

Table of Contents

16

24

66

Introduction

Learn to knit cables without qualms!
Jill Wright demystifies those alluring curves so that
beginners no longer have to feel intimidated.

You'll start out making a simple sample cable and then move on to
10 projects that help you learn a little more as you make each one.
The patterns have complete explanations, and all along the way,
we also have free online technique videos to help you; just look for
this camera icon 🎥 and go to **www.leisurearts.com/5648**. Have fun
knitting all the lovely cables — without fear!

MEET THE DESIGNER
Jill Wright

Jill Wright is a firm believer in challenging
oneself and trying to overcome one's fears.
She created the designs in this book to help knitters
realize that cable patterns are not as difficult as they might look. "My
Mother taught me to knit at age 6, and I have always loved cables —
the more complex the better."
Jill was born and raised in Newcastle Upon Tyne, England, but now
lives in Colorado with her husband and three active sons.
Jill says, "I love to make all things — from scarves to socks, bags to
sweaters, hats to shawls. As long as I'm knitting something, I'm happy."
Her knit and crochet designs have been published in numerous top
magazines and books. For more about Jill, visit her website,
www.woolcrafting.com, or look for her as Woolcrafter on Ravelry.com.

Let's Get Started

A basic maneuver is used for all Cables, from the most intricate braids to the most simple Twists, just a switching of the positions of the cable stitches. There are different ways to accomplish this, but using a cable needle is the simplest.

Let's start by knitting the cable used in the Belt and the Scarf—a Cable 4 Back. The name of the cable tells you two things; **how many** stitches are involved (4) and **where** the stitches on the cable needle will be held (in the back).

The first half of the stitches for any cable are the "moving" or "held" stitches. For this sample, the first two cable stitches will be moved to a cable needle and put "on hold," while the second half of the stitches are being worked from the left needle.

Enough with the conversation!
It's time to knit cables.
You will need some materials: straight knitting needles, size 8 (5 mm), a cable needle of your choice (*see Cable Needles, page* 11) and medium weight yarn.

Make a
Sample Cable

Once you have made this little cable strip, you will be able to make any of the projects in this book using the same principles. Watch this sample being knit online at www.leisurearts.com/5648. You'll learn a lot!

Cast on 10 stitches.

Row 1 (Right side)**:** Slip 1 as if to **knit**, P2, K4, P3.

Row 2: Slip 1 as if to **purl**, K2, P4, K3.

The next row is a Cable 4 Back row.

Row 3 (Cable row)**:**
Step 1 - Slip 1 as if to **knit**, P2.

Step 2 - Slip the next 2 stitches onto the cable needle (**Fig. 1**).

Fig. 1

Step 3 - Move the cable needle to the **back** of your work **(Fig. 2)**.

Fig. 2

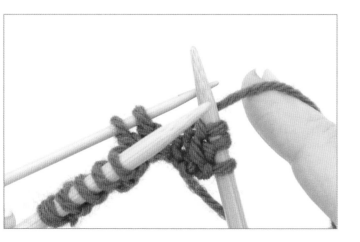

Step 4 - Knit the next 2 stitches on the left needle **(Fig. 3)**.

Fig. 3

Step 5 - Knit the 2 stitches from the cable needle **(Fig. 4)**, making sure that they are worked in the same order as they were slipped onto the cable needle (*cable shown in Fig. 5*).

Fig. 4

Fig. 5

Step 6 - Purl the last 3 stitches on the left needle.

It may not look like it at this point but you have just made a cable. **Keep going** — it's going to grow and transform before your eyes!

My rule of thumb is to add 1 to the number of the cable stitches to find the number of rows to work between the cable rows. Since this cable uses 4 stitches, work the next 5 rows as follows:

Row 4: Slip 1 as if to **purl**, K2, P4, K3.

Row 5: Slip 1 as if to **knit**, P2, K4, P3.

Rows 6-8: Repeat Rows 4 and 5 once, then repeat Row 4 once **more**.

It's time to work the cable row again.

Row 9 (Cable row)**:** Repeat Row 3 to complete another Cable 4 Back (**Fig. 6**).

Fig. 6

Rows 10-14: Repeat Rows 4-8.

Since you have worked the 5 rows that go between a 4 stitch cable, let's work a new kind of cable, a Cable 4 Front, like the one in the Car Seat Cover, page 44. The next row will be the cable row.

Row 15 (Cable row)**:**
Step 1 - Slip 1 as if to **knit**, P2.

Step 2 - Slip the next 2 stitches onto the cable needle (**Fig. 7**).

Fig. 7

Step 3 - Move the cable needle to the **front** of your work (**Fig. 8**).

Fig. 8

Step 4 - Knit the next 2 stitches on the left needle (**Fig. 9**).

Fig. 9

Step 5 - Knit the 2 stitches from the cable needle (**Fig. 10**), making sure that they are worked in the same order as they were slipped onto the cable needle (*cable shown in Fig. 11*).

Fig. 10

Fig. 11

Step 6 - Purl the last 3 stitches on the left needle.

Rows 16-20: Repeat Rows 4-8.

The next row is a cable row.

Row 21 (Cable row)**:** Repeat Row 15 to complete another Cable 4 Front.

Rows 22-25: Repeat Rows 4 and 5 twice.

Bind off all stitches in pattern.

Ta-da!

You just completed the Sample Cable. Now you are ready for any cable in this book! If you are interested in learning how to work from a chart, turn to page 10. A complete chart of the Sample Cable is included.

Reading A Chart

A chart will illustrate how the stitches will look from the right side of a pattern using symbols. The key will include what each symbol represents. As there can be differences in symbols from chart to chart, be sure to look for definitions in the key. Note the row numbers on the sides of the chart. When knitting flat (in rows), a chart is followed from **right** to **left** on **right** side rows and from **left** to **right** on **wrong** side rows. If you are knitting in the round as in the Hat, page 30, all the round numbers will be at the right edge of the chart as the right side will be always facing you.

You worked two different cables in your Sample Cable, both using 4 stitches. The Back Cable symbol on Rows 3 and 9 shows the moving stitches (the first 2 stitches) **behind** the next 2 stitches. The Front Cable symbol on Rows 15 and 21 shows the moving stitches in **front** of the next 2 stitches. The slant of the stitches on the front of the work shows why a front cable can be also named a left cable and a back cable called a right cable.

With a pattern that has each stitch charted like this sample or like the Belt, page 16, you could knit the project by following the chart instead of the written instructions, beginning by casting on the required number of stitches. In other projects, the cabled area will be all that is charted.

A great way to keep your place on a chart is to place a sticky note immediately above the row that you are following. Use 2 sticky notes, one above and one below, if you need more help in keeping on the right track.

CHART

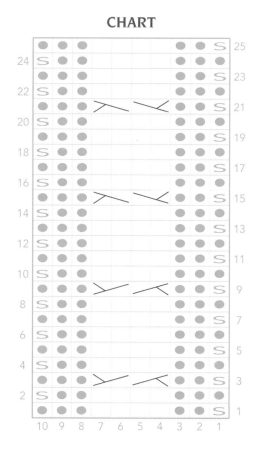

KEY

	Knit on **right** side, purl on **wrong** side
●	Purl on **right** side, knit on **wrong** side
S	Slip 1 as if to **knit** on **right** side, slip 1 as if to **purl** on **wrong** side

Cable 4 Back (*abbreviated* **C4B**)

Cable 4 Front (*abbreviated* **C4F**)

On **right** side rows, follow chart from **right** to **left**; on **wrong** side rows, follow chart from **left** to **right**.

Cable Needles

Cable needles are all double pointed and come in three basic shapes: straight, straight with a dip in the middle, and a bent J-shape. They are made in different sizes to match the weight of the yarn: thick for bulkier yarn and thin for lighter yarn.

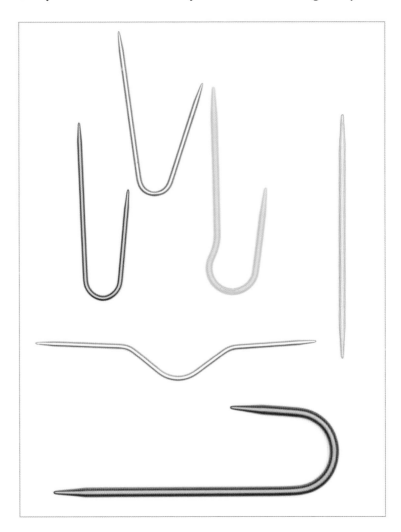

Another Way To Work A Cable

📹 Watch the video of this technique online at www.leisurearts.com/5648. The truly adventurous can work cables without a cable needle. This technique works well with 4 to 6 stitch cables. Instead of slipping the stitches to a cable needle, they are removed from the left needle, then slipped back onto the left needle in their new positions so that all you have to do is knit them.

SAMPLE CABLE

Cast on 10 stitches.

Row 1 (Right side)**:** Slip 1 as if to **knit**, P2, K4, P3.

Row 2: Slip 1 as if to **purl**, K2, P4, K3.

Work a Cable 4 Back without a cable needle as follows:

Row 3 (Cable row)**:**
Step 1 - Slip 1 as if to **knit**, P2.

Step 2 - Skip the next 2 stitches on the left needle and slip the right needle as if to **purl** into the front of the next 2 stitches (**Fig. 12**).

Fig. 12

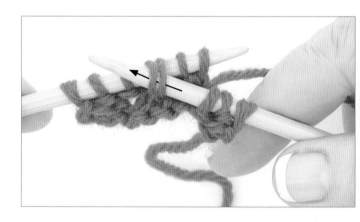

Step 3 - Hold all 4 stitches with your right forefinger and thumb (**Fig. 13**).

Fig. 13

Step 4 - Leaving the right needle in the 2 stitches, slip all 4 stitches off the left needle.

Step 5 - Insert the left needle into the 2 stitches hanging loose (**Fig. 14**).

Fig. 14

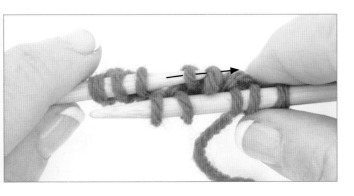

Step 6 - Slip the 2 stitches on the right needle back to the left needle (**Fig. 15**).

Fig. 15

Step 7 - Knit the 4 stitches of the cable (**Fig. 16**).

Fig. 16

Step 8 - Purl the last 3 stitches.

Row 4: Slip 1 as if to **purl**, K2, P4, K3.

Row 5: Slip 1 as if to **knit**, P2, K4, P3.

Rows 6-8: Repeat Rows 4 and 5 once, then repeat Row 4 once **more**.

The next row is a cable row.

Row 9 (Cable row)**:** Repeat Row 3 to complete another Cable 4 Back.

Rows 10-14: Repeat Rows 4-8.

Now, work a Cable 4 Front without a cable needle.

Row 15 (Cable row)**:**
Step 1 - Slip 1 as if to **knit**, P2.

Step 2 - Skip the next 2 stitches on the left needle and insert the right needle into the **back** of the next 2 stitches **(Fig. 17)**.

Fig. 17

Step 3 - Hold all 4 stitches with your right forefinger and thumb.

Step 4 - Leaving the right needle in the 2 stitches, slip all 4 stitches off the left needle **(Fig. 18)**.

Fig. 18

Step 5 - Insert the left needle into the 2 stitches hanging loose **(Fig. 19)**.

Fig. 19

Step 6 - Slip the 2 stitches on the right needle back to the left needle **(Fig. 20)**.

Fig. 20

Step 7 - Knit the 4 stitches of the cable **(Fig. 21)**.

Fig. 21

Step 8 - Purl the last 3 stitches.

Rows 16-20: Repeat Rows 4-8

The next row is a cable row.

Row 21 (Cable row)**:** Repeat Row 15 to complete another Cable 4 Front.

Rows 22-26: Repeat Rows 4-8

Bind off all stitches in pattern.

Belt

This classic belt is a cinch to knit and a great confidence builder for a beginner. The narrow project is super easy, featuring two identical cables running side by side. Follow the chart and instructions to knit the six-row repeat until your belt is the correct length. Add the buckle and you're done!

Belt

● ■ ☐☐ **EASY**

Finished Size: 1½" wide x 36" long (3.75 cm x 91.5 cm)

SHOPPING LIST

Yarn (Light Weight)
[1.75 ounces, 123 yards
(50 grams, 113 meters) per ball]:
☐ 1 ball

Knitting Needles
Straight,
☐ Size 3 (3.25 mm)
   or size needed for gauge

Additional Supplies
☐ Cable needle
☐ Tapestry needle
☐ 1½" (4 cm) Buckle

GAUGE INFORMATION

In pattern, 13 sts = 1½" (3.75 cm)

STITCH GUIDE

CABLE 4 BACK (*abbreviated* **C4B**)
Slip 2 sts onto cable needle and hold in
back of work, K2 from left needle, K2
from cable needle.

INSTRUCTIONS

Cast on 13 sts.

Repeat Chart Rows 1-6 (*see Reading A Chart, page 10*) or follow instructions below until Belt measures approximately 36" (91.5 cm) from cast on edge, ending by working Row 6.

Row 1 (Right side): Slip 1 as if to **knit**, K4, P1, K1, P1, K5.

Row 2: Slip 1 as if to **purl**, P4, K1, P1, K1, P5.

Row 3: Slip 1 as if to **knit**, C4B, P1, K1, P1, C4B, K1.

Row 4: Repeat Row 2.

Rows 5 and 6: Repeat Rows 1 and 2.

Repeat Rows 1-6 until Belt measures approximately 36" (91.5 cm) from cast on edge, ending by working Row 6.

Bind off all sts in **knit**, leaving a long end for sewing.

With **right** side facing, slide buckle ½" (12 mm) onto bound off end of Belt, pushing the prong through center stitch. Fold end to **wrong** side and sew in place.

CHART

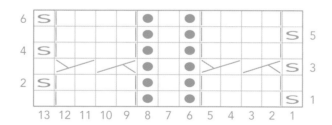

KEY

☐ Knit on **right** side, purl on **wrong** side

● Purl on **right** side, knit on **wrong** side

Ⓢ Slip 1 as if to **knit** on **right** side, slip 1 as if to **purl** on **wrong** side

⤬⤫ C4B

On **right** side rows, follow Chart from **right** to **left**; on **wrong** side rows, follow Chart from **left** to **right**.

Scarf

For this pretty scarf, you will be using
the same cable stitch as you did for the
belt. The main difference is that you will
be working a narrow section of ribbing
in between the two cables and along
each edge. This easy project is sure to
become a favorite for accenting your
wardrobe and making gifts.

Scarf

Finished Size: 4" wide x 53" long (10 cm x 134.5 cm)

SHOPPING LIST

Yarn (Medium Weight) **4**

[3 ounces, 197 yards

(85 grams, 180 meters) per skein]:

☐ 2 skeins

Knitting Needles

Straight,

☐ Size 8 (5 mm) **or** size needed for gauge

Additional Supplies

☐ Cable needle

GAUGE INFORMATION

In pattern, 32 sts = 4" (10 cm)

——STITCH GUIDE——

CABLE 4 BACK (*abbreviated* C4B)

Slip 2 sts onto cable needle and hold in **back** of work, K2 from left needle, K2 from cable needle.

INSTRUCTIONS

Cast on 32 sts.

Repeat Chart Rows 1-6 (*see Reading A Chart, page 10*) or follow instructions below until Scarf measures approximately 53" (134.5 cm) from cast on edge, ending by working Row 1.

Row 1 (Right side): Slip 1 as if to **knit**, K2, P2, C4B, P2, (K2, P2) 3 times, C4B, P2, K3.

Row 2: Slip 1 as if to **purl**, P2, K2, P4, K2, (P2, K2) 3 times, P4, K2, P3.

Row 3: Slip 1 as if to **knit**, K2, P2, K4, P2, (K2, P2) 3 times, K4, P2, K3.

Rows 4-6: Repeat Rows 2 and 3 once, then repeat Row 2 once **more**.

Repeat Rows 1-6 for pattern until Scarf measures approximately 53" (134.5 cm) from cast on edge, ending by working Row 1.

Bind off all sts in pattern.

CHART

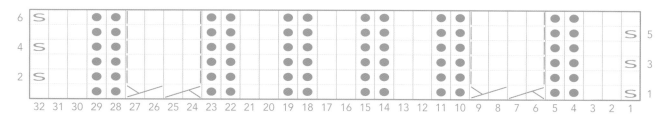

KEY

☐ Knit on **right** side, purl on **wrong** side

⬤ Purl on **right** side, knit on **wrong** side

S Slip 1 as if to **knit** on **right** side, slip 1 as if to **purl** on **wrong** side

⋉⋊ C4B

On **right** side rows, follow Chart from **right** to **left**;
on **wrong** side rows, follow Chart from **left** to **right**.

Felted Clutch

Felting makes this project look special, but it is actually simple to knit in mostly stockinette stitch pattern with a wide cable down the center. If you are new to felting, be sure and notice that you should avoid using a superwash wool, because it won't felt properly. Also, you will have to work with separate balls of yarn for a few rows to create a vertical slit for the buttonhole.

Felted Clutch

■■■◻ **INTERMEDIATE**

Finished Size:

Approximately 12" wide x 27" long (30.5 cm x 68.5 cm) (before sewing and felting)

Approximately 10½" wide x 6" deep (26.5 cm x 15 cm) (after sewing and felting)

SHOPPING LIST

Yarn (100% Wool Medium Weight) [MEDIUM 4]

[3.5 ounces, 210 yards (100 grams, 192 meters) per skein]:

☐ 2 skeins

Note: Avoid wool yarn that is superwash as it will **not** felt.

Knitting Needles

Straight,

☐ Size 7 (4.5 mm) **or** size needed for gauge

Additional Supplies

☐ Cable needle

☐ Yarn needle

☐ 1½" (4 cm) Button

☐ Sewing needle and matching thread

GAUGE INFORMATION

In pattern,

22 sts and 25 rows = 4" (10 cm)

── STITCH GUIDE ──

CABLE 8 FRONT

(*abbreviated* C8F)

Slip 4 sts onto cable needle and hold in **front** of work, K4 from left needle, K4 from cable needle.

INSTRUCTIONS
BODY

Cast on 66 sts.

Row 1 (Right side)**:** K 26, P3, K8, P3, knit across.

Row 2: P 26, K3, P8, K3, purl across.

Rows 3 and 4: Repeat Rows 1 and 2.

Row 5: K 26, P3, C8F, P3, knit across.

Row 6: P 26, K3, P8, K3, purl across.

Rows 7-10: Repeat Rows 1 and 2 twice.

Repeat Rows 1-10 for pattern until Body measures approximately 25" (63.5 cm) from cast on edge, ending by working Row 6.

CHART

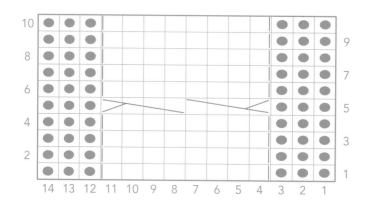

KEY

☐ Knit on **right** side, purl on **wrong** side

⬤ Purl on **right** side, knit on **wrong** side

▱ C8F

On **right** side rows, follow Chart from **right** to **left**; on **wrong** side rows, follow Chart from **left** to **right**.

BUTTONHOLE

Both sides of the Buttonhole are worked at the same time, using separate balls of yarn.

Row 1: K 26, P3, K4; with second yarn, K4, P3, knit across.

Row 2: P 26, K3, P4; with second yarn, P4, K3, purl across.

Row 3: K 26, P3, K4; with second yarn, K4, P3, knit across.

Rows 4-6: Repeat Rows 2 and 3 once, then repeat Row 2 once **more**.

Row 7: K 26, P3, K4, cut yarn; with remaining yarn, K4, P3, knit across.

Row 8 (Joining row)**:** P 26, K3, P8, K3, purl across.

Rows 9-14: Repeat Body Rows 5-10.

Bind off all sts in pattern.

With **wrong** side facing, fold up cast on end 8" (20.5 cm) and sew each side seam.

FELTING

Place the clutch in a zippered pillowcase or mesh laundry bag. Set your washing machine to HOT water on the smallest load size with a regular cycle. Add approximately 1 tablespoon of a wool friendly detergent. Add a pair of well-washed but not ragged jeans for extra agitation. DO NOT ALLOW WASHER TO SPIN – spinning may form creases in felting, which cannot be removed. Remove clutch at the end of the wash cycle. Rinse by hand in cool/cold water and allow to air dry.

Sew button close to bottom fold on center Body to correspond with buttonhole.

Hat

For this perky hat, you'll be working in the round with a circular needle. The pattern alternates a simple cable with a twist, which is basically a mini cable using only two stitches. When you're finished, knit a drawstring cord to weave through the spaces formed by the last round of cables. If you're feeling sassy, you can even pull your ponytail through the top opening!

Hat

■■■□ INTERMEDIATE

Finished Size: 20" circumference x 8" high (51 cm x 20.5 cm)

SHOPPING LIST

Yarn (Light Weight)

[1.75 ounces, 144 yards
(50 grams, 133 meters) per hank]:
☐ 2 hanks

Knitting Needles

16" (40.5 cm) Circular knitting needle,
☐ Size 6 (4 mm) **or** size needed for gauge
Double pointed needles,
☐ Size 6 (4 mm) - 2

Additional Supplies

☐ Cable needle
☐ Marker

GAUGE INFORMATION

In pattern, 26 sts and 36 rows = 4" (10 cm)

TECHNIQUE USED

• K2 tog (**Fig. 25, page 89**)

🎥 This Hat features a mini cable called a Left Twist. You can either use your cable needle to work the stitch or follow the instructions on the next page to knit the stitches from the left needle to twist them. Watch both techniques at www.leisurearts.com/5648.

STITCH GUIDE

CABLE 6 FRONT (*abbreviated* C6F)

Slip 3 sts onto cable needle and hold in **front** of work, K3 from left needle, K3 from cable needle.

LEFT TWIST (*abbreviated* LT)

Slip 1 st onto cable needle and hold in **front** of work, K1 from left needle, K1 from cable needle **OR** knit into the **back** of the second stitch on left needle (**Fig. A**), then **knit** the first stitch (**Fig. B**), letting both stitches drop off the needle at the same time.

Fig. A

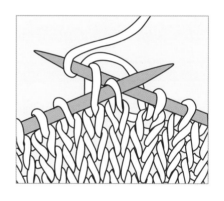

Fig. B

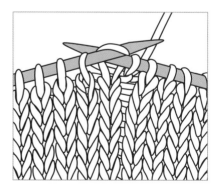

CHART

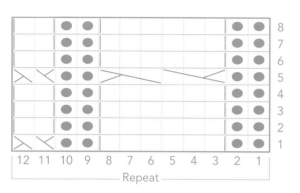

KEY

☐ Knit

● Purl

⤬ LT

⤬ C6F

Follow Chart from **right** to **left**.

INSTRUCTIONS
BODY

Using circular needle, cast on 132 sts; place marker to indicate beginning of rnd (*see Markers, page 87*).

Repeat Chart Rnds 1-8, page 33 (*see Reading a Chart, page 10*) or follow instructions below until Body measures approximately 8" (20.5 cm) from cast on edge, ending by working Rnd 8.

Rnd 1: ★ P2, K6, P2, LT; repeat from ★ around.

Rnds 2-4: ★ P2, K6, P2, K2; repeat from ★ around.

Rnd 5: ★ P2, C6F, P2, LT; repeat from ★ around.

Rnds 6-8: ★ P2, K6, P2, K2; repeat from ★ around.

Repeat Rnds 1-8 for pattern until Body measures approximately 8" (20.5 cm) from cast on edge, ending by working Row 8.

Bind off all sts in pattern.

CORD
Using a double pointed needle, cast on 4 sts.

Row 1: K4, slide sts to opposite end of needle.

Repeat Row 1 until Cord measures approximately 30" (76 cm) from cast on edge.

Next Row: K2 tog twice, slide sts to opposite end of needle: 2 sts.

Last Row: K2 tog: one st.

Cut yarn and pull end through last st.

Weave Cord through spaces formed by cables on the last Rnd 5 worked.

USING CIRCULAR KNITTING NEEDLES

Cast on all the stitches as instructed. Untwist and straighten the stitches on the needle to be sure that the cast on ridge lies on the inside of the needle and never rolls around the needle.

Hold the needle so that the ball of yarn is attached to the stitch closest to the right hand point. Place a marker to mark the beginning of the round. To begin working in the round, work the stitches on the left hand point as instructed (**Fig. C**).

Continue working each round as instructed **without turning the work**; but for the first three rounds or so, check to be sure that the cast on has not twisted around the needle. If it has, it is impossible to untwist it. The only way to fix this is to rip it out and return to the cast on row.

(**Fig. C**)

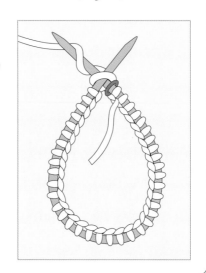

Fingerless Gloves

By now, you have seen how cables can be made to turn in different directions. This is determined by whether the stitches are held to the front or the back as you make the cable. These Fingerless Gloves are designed to be symmetrical, with their cables going in opposite directions. Three sizes are given, and color coding is used to make the instructions easier to follow.

Fingerless Gloves

■■■□ INTERMEDIATE

SIZE INFORMATION

Size	To Fit Palm Circumference
Small	6½" (16.5 cm)
Medium	7¼" (18.5 cm)
Large	8" (20.5 cm)

Size Note: We have printed the instructions in different colors to make it easier for you to find:

• Size Small in Blue
• Size Medium in Pink
• Size Large in Green

Instructions in Black apply to all sizes.

GAUGE INFORMATION

In Stockinette Stitch

　(knit one row, purl one row),

　22 sts and 30 rows = 4" (10 cm)

————STITCH GUIDE————

CABLE 8 FRONT (*abbreviated* C8F)

Slip 4 sts onto cable needle and hold in **front** of work, K4 from left needle, K4 from cable needle.

CABLE 8 BACK (*abbreviated* C8B)

Slip 4 sts onto cable needle and hold in **back** of work, K4 from left needle, K4 from cable needle.

LEFT GLOVE CHART

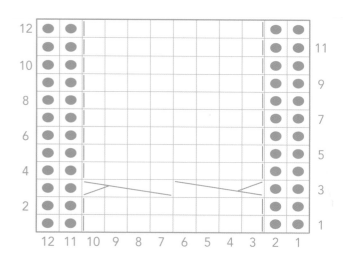

KEY

On **right** side rows, follow Chart from **right** to **left**; on **wrong** side rows, follow Chart from **left** to **right**.

INSTRUCTIONS
LEFT GLOVE

Leaving a long end for sewing, cast on 40{44-48} sts.

Work in K1, P1 ribbing until Glove measures approximately 1½" (4 cm) from cast on edge.

Body

Row 1: K 6{8-10}, P2, K8, P2, K 22{24-26}.

Row 2: P 22{24-26}, K2, P8, K2, P 6{8-10}.

Row 3: K 6{8-10}, P2, C8F, P2, K 22{24-26}.

Row 4: P 22{24-26}, K2, P8, K2, P 6{8-10}.

Rows 5-12: Repeat Rows 1 and 2, 4 times.

Repeat Rows 3-12 for pattern until Glove measures approximately 8½" (21.5 cm) from cast on edge, ending by working Row 6.

Work in K1, P1 ribbing for 1" (2.5 cm).

Bind off all sts in ribbing, leaving a long end for sewing.

RIGHT GLOVE

Leaving a long end for sewing, cast on 40{44-48} sts.

Work in K1, P1 ribbing until Glove measures approximately 1½" (4 cm) from cast on edge.

Body

Row 1: K 22{24-26}, P2, K8, P2, K 6{8-10}.

Row 2: P 6{8-10}, K2, P8, K2, P 22{24-26}.

Row 3: K 22{24-26}, P2, C8B, P2, K 6{8-10}.

Row 4: P 6{8-10}, K2, P8, K2, P 22{24-26}.

Rows 5-10: Repeat Rows 1 and 2, 4 times.

Repeat Rows 13-12 until Glove measures approximately approximately 8½" (21.5 cm) from cast on edge, ending by working Row 6.

Work in K1, P1 ribbing 1" (2.5 cm).

Bind off all sts in ribbing, leaving a long end for sewing.

Thread tapestry needle with long end on bind off edge of one Glove. Weave seam for 2" (5 cm) **(Fig. 31, page 91)**. Thread tapestry needle with long end from cast on edge and weave remainder of seam, leaving a 2" (5 cm) gap for thumb opening.

Repeat for remaining Glove.

RIGHT GLOVE CHART

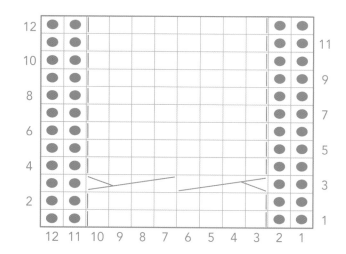

KEY

☐ Knit on **right** side, purl on **wrong** side

● Purl on **right** side, knit on **wrong** side

⟋⟍ C8B

On **right** side rows, follow Chart from **right** to **left**; on **wrong** side rows, follow Chart from **left** to **right**.

Car Seat Cover

This little throw will keep Baby's legs warm in a car seat or other carrier. Cables accent the edges of the pretty textured center section. Notice that what looks like a wider cable is actually formed by working a front cable beside a back cable of the same width, merging the two cables into a "horseshoe" effect.

Car Seat Cover

Finished Size: 22" (56 cm) square

SHOPPING LIST

Yarn (Light Weight)
[5 ounces, 362 yards
(140 grams, 331 meters) per skein]:
☐ 2 skeins

Knitting Needles
24" (61 cm) Circular knitting needle,
☐ Size 7 (4.5 mm) **or** size needed for gauge

Additional Supplies
☐ Cable needle
☐ Markers

GAUGE INFORMATION
In center pattern, 21 sts and 32 rows = 4" (10 cm)

STITCH GUIDE

CABLE 4 BACK (*abbreviated* C4B)
Slip 2 sts onto cable needle and hold in
back of work, K2 from left needle, K2 from
cable needle.

CABLE 4 FRONT (*abbreviated* C4F)
Slip 2 sts onto cable needle and hold in **front**
of work, K2 from left needle, K2 from cable
needle.

INSTRUCTIONS

Cast on 128 sts.

Rows 1-3: Knit across.

Row 4: K2, P2, K4, P2, K8, P2, place marker, (K1, P1) 44 times, place marker, P2, K8, P2, K4, P2, K2.

Row 5: P2, K2, P4, K2, P8, K2, (K1, P1) across to next marker, K2, P8, K2, P4, K2, P2.

Row 6: K2, P2, K4, P2, K8, P2, (P1, K1) across to next marker, P2, K8, P2, K4, P2, K2.

Row 7: P2, K2, P4, K2, P8, K2, (P1, K1) across to next marker, K2, P8, K2, P4, K2, P2.

Row 8: K2, (P2, C4B) twice, C4F, P2, (K1, P1) across to next marker, P2, C4B, (C4F, P2) twice, K2.

Rows 9-11: Repeat Rows 5-7.

Repeat Rows 8-11 for pattern until Cover measures approximately 21½" (54.5 cm) from cast on edge, ending by working Row 7.

Last 3 Rows: Knit across.

Bind off all sts in **knit**.

LEFT SIDE CHART

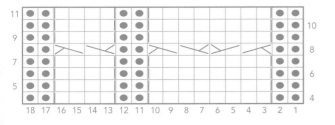

RIGHT SIDE CHART

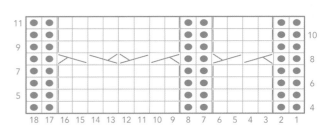

KEY

☐ Knit on **right** side, purl on **wrong** side

⊡ Purl on **right** side, knit on **wrong** side

▷◁▭◁ C4B

▷◁▭◁ C4F

On **right** side rows, follow Chart from **right** to **left**;
on **wrong** side rows, follow Chart from **left** to **right**.

Cushion

When you alternate front and back cables, the pattern forms a true braid. That is what creates the rich look of the cables on this cushion. The easy project is made all in one piece and wrapped around a pillow form. Side seams and a button closure keep the cover in place.

Cushion

■■■□ INTERMEDIATE

Finished Size: 16" wide x 37" long (40.5 cm x 91.5 cm) (before sewing)

SHOPPING LIST

Yarn (Bulky Weight) **BULKY 5**
[3.5 ounces, 120 yards
(100 grams, 109 meters) per ball]:
☐ 4 balls

Knitting Needles
Straight,
☐ Size 10 (6 mm) **or** size needed for gauge

Additional Supplies
☐ Cable needle
☐ Yarn needle
☐ Pins
☐ 18" (45.5 cm) Square pillow form
☐ 1½" (4 cm) Button
☐ Sewing needle and matching thread

GAUGE INFORMATION
In P3, K2 ribbing, 12 sts and 19 rows = 4" (10 cm)

CABLE 6 FRONT (*abbreviated* **C6F**)

Slip 3 sts onto cable needle and hold in **front** of work, K3 from left needle, K3 from cable needle.

CABLE 6 BACK (*abbreviated* **C6B**)

Slip 3 sts onto cable needle and hold in **back** of work, K3 from left needle, K3 from cable needle.

CABLE 12 FRONT (*abbreviated* **C12F**)

Slip 6 sts onto cable needle and hold in **front** of work, K6 from left needle, K6 from cable needle.

CABLE 12 BACK (*abbreviated* **C12B**)

Slip 6 sts onto cable needle and hold in **back** of work, K6 from left needle, K6 from cable needle.

SIDE CABLE

Row 1: K9.

Row 2 AND ALL EVEN NUMBERED ROWS: P9.

Row 3: K3, C6F.

Row 5: K9.

Row 7: C6B, K3.

Row 8: P9.

Repeat Rows 1-8 for pattern.

CENTER CABLE

Row 1: K 18.

Row 2 AND ALL EVEN NUMBERED ROWS: P 18.

Rows 3 and 5: K 18.

Row 7: K6, C12F.

Rows 9, 11, and 13: K 18.

Row 15: C12B, K6.

Row 16: P 18.

Repeat Rows 1-16 for pattern.

SIDE CABLE CHART

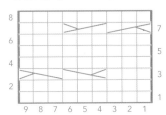

CENTER CABLE CHART

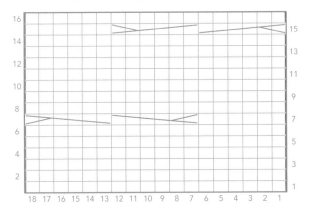

KEY

☐ Knit on **right** side, purl on **wrong** side

C6F

C6B

C12F

C12B

On **right** side rows, follow Chart from **right** to **left**; on **wrong** side rows, follow Chart from **left** to **right**.

INSTRUCTIONS

Cast on 60 sts.

Rows 1-3: Knit across.

Row 4: K2, P2, work Row 1 of Side Cable, P3, K2, P3, work Row 1 of Center Cable, P3, K2, P3, work Row 1 of Side Cable, P2, K2.

Row 5: P2, K2, work next row of Side Cable, K3, P2, K3, work next row of Center Cable, K3, P2, K3, work next row of Side Cable, K2, P2.

Row 6: K2, P2, work next row of Side Cable, P3, K2, P3, work next row of Center Cable, P3, K2, P3, work next row of Side Cable, P2, K2.

Repeat Rows 5 and 6 until Cover measures approximately 37" (94 cm) from cast on edge, ending by working Row 16 of Center Cable.

Buttonhole Row: Continue in established pattern across first 28 sts, bind off next 4 sts, work across.

Next Row: Work across to bound off sts, **turn**; add on 4 sts (**Figs. 23a & b, page 88**), **turn**; work across.

Bind off all sts in pattern.

Finishing

With **wrong** side together, wrap Cover around pillow form, overlapping the last 3 rows and the first 3 rows. Pin side edges together and remove form. Weave side seams (**Fig. 31, page 91**). Sew button opposite buttonhole. Insert form.

Vest

What a difference a cable can
make! With a single cable on
each side of the front, this
vest takes on extra fashion
appeal. A cabled tab adds
interest to the back.

Vest

◼◼◼◻ **INTERMEDIATE**

SIZE INFORMATION

Size	Finished Chest Measurement
X-Small	33½" (85 cm)
Small	37½" (95.5 cm)
Medium	42" (106.5 cm)
Large	46½" (118 cm)
X-Large	50½" (128.5 cm)
2X-Large	54½" (138.5 cm)

Size Note: We have printed the instructions in different colors to make it easier for you to find:

- **Size X-Small in Purple**
- **Size Small in Blue**
- **Size Medium in Pink**
- Size Large in Lime
- **Size X-Large in Dark Blue**
- **Size 2X-Large in Green**

Instructions in Black apply to all sizes.

.

SHOPPING LIST

Yarn (Medium Weight)

[1.75 ounces, 189 yards (50 grams, 173 meters) per hank]:

☐ {7-8-9}{10-11-11} hanks

Knitting Needles

Straight,

☐ Size 7 (4.5 mm) **or** size needed for gauge

Additional Supplies

☐ Cable needle

☐ Markers

☐ Yarn needle

☐ Hook and loop closure - 2

GAUGE INFORMATION

In Reverse Stockinette Stitch
(purl one row, knit one row),
20 sts and 32 rows = 4" (10 cm)

TECHNIQUES USED

- M1 (**Figs. 22a & b, page 88**)
- K2 tog (**Fig. 25, page 89**)
- SSK (**Figs. 26a-c, page 89**)
- P2 tog (**Fig. 27, page 90**)
- P2 tog tbl (**Fig. 28, page 90**)

STITCH GUIDE

CABLE 8 BACK (*abbreviated* **C8B**)

Slip 4 sts onto cable needle and hold in **back** of work, K4 from left needle, K4 from cable needle.

CABLE 8 FRONT (*abbreviated* **C8F**)

Slip 4 sts onto cable needle and hold in **front** of work, K4 from left needle, K4 from cable needle.

LEFT FRONT CABLE

Row 1: P 12.

Row 2: K4, C8F.

Row 3: P 12.

Row 4: K 12.

Row 5: P 12.

Row 6: C8B, K4.

Rows 7 and 8: Repeat Rows 3 and 4.

Repeat Rows 1-8 for pattern.

RIGHT FRONT CABLE

Row 1: P 12.

Row 2: C8B, K4.

Row 3: P 12.

Row 4: K 12.

Row 5: P 12.

Row 6: K4, C8F.

Rows 7 and 8: Repeat Rows 3 and 4.

Repeat Rows 1-8 for pattern.

LEFT FRONT CHART

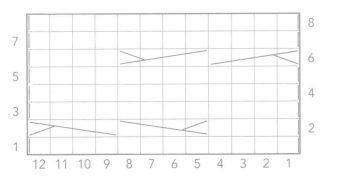

RIGHT FRONT CHART

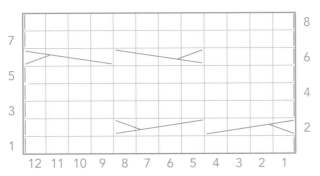

KEY

Knit on **right** side, purl on **wrong** side

C8B

C8F

On **right** side rows, follow Chart from **right** to **left**; on **wrong** side rows, follow Chart from **left** to **right**.

INSTRUCTIONS
Back

Cast on {90-100-110}
{120-130-140} sts.

Row 1: (K1, P1) across.

Row 2: (P1, K1) across.

Rows 3-8: Repeat Rows 1
and 2, 3 times.

Body

Row 1 (Right side)**:** Purl across.

Row 2: Knit across.

Repeat Rows 1 and 2 until
Back measures approximately
{18-18-18}{19-19-19}"/
{45.5-45.5-45.5}{48.5-48.5-48.5} cm
from cast on edge, ending
by working a **wrong** side row.

Armhole Shaping

Rows 1 and 2: Bind off
{5-6-7}{9-10-10} sts, work across:
{80-88-96}{102-110-120} sts.

Row 3: Slip 1 as if to **purl**,
(P1, K1) 3 times, P2 tog tbl,
purl across to last 9 sts, P2 tog,
K1, (P1, K1) 3 times: {78-86-94}
{100-108-118} sts.

Row 4 (Decrease row)**:** Slip 1 as
if to **purl**, (P1, K1) 3 times, SSK,
knit across to last 9 sts, K2 tog,
K1, (P1, K1) 3 times: {76-84-92}
{98-106-116} sts.

Row 5: Slip 1 as if to **purl**,
(P1, K1) 3 times, purl across to
last 7 sts, K1, (P1, K1) 3 times.

Repeat Rows 4 and 5, {4-5-7}
{7-8-9} times: {68-74-78}
{84-90-98} sts.

Work even until Armholes
measures approximately
{7-7½-8}{8½-9-9}"/{18-19-20.5}
{21.5-23-23} cm, ending by
working a **right** side row.

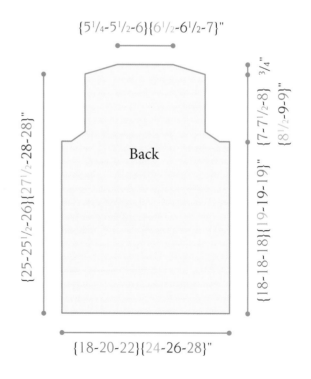

{5¼-5½-6}{6½-6½-7}"

{25-25½-26}{27½-28-28}"

Back

{18-18-18}{19-19-19}"

{7-7½-8}{8½-9-9}"

¾"

{18-20-22}{24-26-28}"

Shoulder Shaping

Maintain established pattern throughout.

Rows 1 and 2: Bind off {7-7-8}{8-9-10} sts at beginning of row, work across: {54-60-62} {68-72-78} sts.

Rows 3-6: Bind off {7-8-8} {9-10-11} sts at beginning of row, work across: {26-28-30} {32-32-34} sts.

Bind off remaining sts in **knit**.

Left Front

BAND

Cast on {44-49-55}{61-66-71} sts.

**SIZES X-SMALL &
X-LARGE ONLY**

Row 1: (K1, P1) across.

Row 2: Slip 1 as if to **purl**,
K1, (P1, K1) across.

Rows 3-8: Repeat Rows 1 and 2,
3 times.

**SIZES SMALL, MEDIUM,
LARGE, & 2X-LARGE ONLY**

Row 1: K1, (P1, K1) across.

Row 2: Slip 1 as if to **purl**,
(P1, K1) across.

Rows 3-8: Repeat Rows 1 and 2,
3 times.

BODY - ALL SIZES

Row 1 (Right side):
P {18-21-25}{29-34-38}, place
marker (*see Markers, page 87*),
(K2, M1) 4 times, place marker,
purl across to last 7 sts, K1, (P1,
K1) 3 times: {48-53-59}
{65-70-75} sts.

Row 2: Slip 1 as if to **purl**, P1,
(K1, P1) twice, knit across to next
marker, work Row 1 of Left Front
Cable, knit across.

Row 3: Purl across to next
marker, work next row of Left
Front Cable, purl across to
last 7 sts, K1, (P1, K1) 3 times.

Row 4: Slip 1 as if to **purl**,
(K1, P1) twice, knit across to next
marker, work next row of Left
Front Cable, knit across.

Repeat Rows 3 and 4 for
pattern until piece measures
approximately {8-8¼-8½}
{9¾-9¾-9¾}"/{20.5-21-21.5}
{25-25-25} cm from cast on
edge, ending by working
a **right** side row.

Neck Shaping

Maintain established pattern
throughout.

Decrease Row: (K1, P1) 3 times,
K2 tog, work across: {47-52-58}
{64-69-74} sts.

Next {9-9-7}{5-7-5} Rows:
Work across.

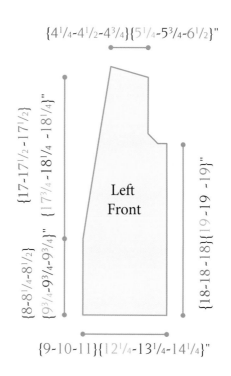

{4¼-4½-4¾}{5¼-5¾-6½}"

{17-17½-17½}"
{17¾-18¼-18¼}"

{18-18-18}{19-19-19}"

Left
Front

{8-8¼-8½}
{9¾-9¾-9¾}"

{9-10-11}{12¼-13¼-14¼}"

Continue to decrease one st at neck edge, every {10th-10th-8th} {6th-8th-6th} row, {1-12-8}{1-16-3} time(s), then decrease every {12th-0-10th}{8th-0-8th} row, {9-0-6}{15-0-14} times (*see Zeros, page 87*), AND AT THE SAME TIME when piece measures same as Back to Armhole Shaping and ending by working a **wrong** side row, work Armhole Shaping as follows:

Row 1: Bind off {5-6-7} {9-10-10} sts, work across.

Row 2: Work across.

Row 3: Slip 1 as if to **purl**, (P1, K1) 3 times, P2 tog tbl, work across.

Row 4 (Decrease row)**:** Work across to last 9 sts, K2 tog, K1, (P1, K1) 3 times.

Row 5: Slip 1 as if to **purl**, (P1, K1) 3 times, work across.

Repeat Rows 4 and 5, {4-5-7}{7-8-9} times.

Continue working established Neck Shaping: {26-27-28} {30-33-36} sts.

Work even until Left Front measures same as Back to Shoulder Shaping, ending by working a **wrong** side row.

Shoulder Shaping

Maintain established pattern throughout.

Row 1: Bind off {5-5-6} {6-7-8} sts, K2 tog, bind off 1 st, work across: {19-20-20} {22-24-26} sts.

Row 2: Work across.

Row 3: Bind off 1 st, K2 tog, bind off {3-4-4}{5-6-7} sts, K2 tog, bind off 1 st, work across: {12-12-12}{13-14-15} sts.

Row 4: Work across.

Row 5: Bind off 2 sts, K2 tog, bind off {4-3-3}{3-2-3} sts, K2 tog, bind off 1 st, work across: {3-4-4}{5-7-7} sts.

Row 6: Work across.

Bind off remaining {3-4-4} {5-7-7} sts in pattern.

Right Front
BAND
Cast on {44-49-55}{61-66-71} sts.

SIZES X-SMALL & X-LARGE ONLY
Row 1: Slip 1 as if to **purl**, P1, (K1, P1) across.

Row 2: (P1, K1) across.

Rows 3-8: Repeat Rows 1 and 2, 3 times.

SIZES SMALL, MEDIUM, LARGE, & 2X-LARGE ONLY
Row 1: Slip 1 as if to **purl**, (P1, K1) across.

Row 2: K1, (P1, K1) across.

Rows 3-8: Repeat Rows 1 and 2, 3 times.

BODY - ALL SIZES
Row 1 (Right side)**:** Slip 1 as -if to **purl**, (P1, K1) 3 times, P {11-13-15}{17-17-18}, place marker, (K2, M1) 4 times, place marker, purl across: {48-53-59} {65-70-75} sts.

Row 2: Knit across to next marker, work Row 1 of Right Front Cable, knit across to last 6 sts, (P1, K1) 3 times.

Row 3: Slip 1 as if to **purl**, (P1, K1) 3 times, purl across to next marker, work next row of Right Front Cable, purl across.

Row 4: Knit across to next marker, work next row of Right Front Cable, knit across to last 6 sts, (P1, K1) 3 times.

Repeat Rows 3 and 4 for pattern until piece measures approximately {8-8¼-8½} {9¾-9¾-9¾}"/{20.5- 21-21.5} {25-25-25} cm from cast on edge, ending by working a **right** side row.

Neck Shaping
Maintain established pattern throughout.

Decrease Row: Work across to last 9 sts, K2 tog, K1, (P1, K1) 3 times: {47-52-58}{64-69-74} sts.

Next {9-9-7}{5-7-5} Rows: Work across.

Continue to decrease one st at neck edge, every {10th-10th-8th} {6th-8th-6th} row, {1-12-8}{1-16-3} time(s), then decrease every {12th-0-10th}{8th-0-8th} row, {9-0-6}{15-0-14} times AND AT THE SAME TIME when piece measures same as Back to Armhole Shaping and ending by working a **right** side row, work Armhole Shaping as follows:

Row 1: Bind off {5-6-7} {9-10-10} sts, work across.

Row 2 (Decrease row): Work across to last 9 sts, P2 tog, K1, (P1, K1) 3 times.

Row 3: Slip 1 as if to **purl**, (P1, K1) 3 times, K2 tog, work across.

Row 4: Work across..

Repeat Rows 3 and 4, {4-5-7}{7-8-9} times.

Continue working established Neck Shaping: {26-27-28}{30-33-36} sts.

Work even until Right Front measures same as Back to Shoulder Shaping, ending by working a **right** side row.

Shoulder Shaping

Maintain established pattern throughout.

Row 1: Bind off {5-5-6}{6-7-8} sts, K2 tog, bind off 1 st, work across: {19-20-20}{22-24-26} sts.

Row 2: Work across.

Row 3: Bind off 1 st, K2 tog, bind off {3-4-4}{5-6-7} sts, K2 tog, bind off 1 st, work across: {12-12-12}{13-14-15} sts.

Row 4: Work across.

Row 5: Bind off 2 sts, K2 tog, bind off {4-3-3}{3-2-3} sts, K2 tog, bind off 1 st, work across: {3-4-4}{5-7-7} sts.

Row 6: Work across.

Bind off remaining {3-4-4}{5-7-7} sts in pattern.

BACK TAB

Cast on 16 sts, leaving a long end for sewing.

Row 1: Slip 1 as if to **knit**, P1, K 12, P1, K1.

Row 2: Slip 1 as if to **purl**, K1, P 12, K1, P1.

Row 3: Slip 1 as if to **knit**, P1, C8B, K4, P1, K1.

Row 4: Slip 1 as if to **purl**, K1, P 12, K1, P1.

Row 5: Slip 1 as if to **knit**, P1, K 12, P1, K1.

Row 6: Slip 1 as if to **purl**, K1, P 12, K1, P1.

Row 7: Slip 1 as if to **knit**, P1, K4, C8F, K6, P1, K1.

Row 8: Repeat Row 4.

Repeat Rows 1-8 for pattern until piece measures {8-8-10} {12-14-14}"/ {20.5-20.5-25.5} {30.5-35.5-35.5} cm from cast on edge, ending by working Row 1.

Bind off all sts in **knit**, leaving a long end for sewing.

FINISHING

Weave side seams (**Fig. 31, page 91**).

Sew shoulder seams.

Center Back Tab at waistline and sew ends in place.

Sew closures to Front waistline.

BACK TAB CHART

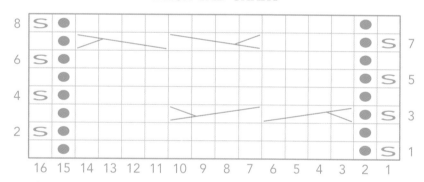

KEY

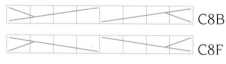 Knit on **right** side, purl on **wrong** side

● Purl on **right** side, knit on **wrong** side

S Slip 1 as if to **knit** on **right** side, slip 1 as if to **purl** on **wrong** side

C8B

C8F

On **right** side rows, follow Chart from **right** to **left**; on **wrong** side rows, follow Chart from **left** to **right**.

Wrap

This soft wrap can double as a shrug
when you button up the edges to form
long sleeves. The background of Reverse
Stockinette Stitch perfectly sets off the
diamond pattern of the large center
cable. Don't be intimidated by the lengthy
instructions and big chart — this cable is
actually a breeze to knit.

Wrap

Finished Size: 18" x 60" (45.5 cm x 152.5 cm)

SHOPPING LIST

Yarn (Medium Weight)
MEDIUM 4
[1.75 ounces, 128 yards
(50 grams, 117 meters) per ball]:

☐ 6 balls

Knitting Needles

Straight,

☐ Size 9 (5.5 mm) **or** size needed for gauge

Additional Supplies

☐ Cable needle

☐ ⁷/₈" (22 mm) Buttons - 10

☐ Sewing needle and matching thread

GAUGE INFORMATION

In Reverse Stockinette Stitch
(purl one row, knit one row),
15 sts and 22 rows = 4" (10 cm)

TECHNIQUES USED

• P2 tog (**Fig. 27**, *page* **90**)
• YO (**Fig. 24**, *page* **89**)

This Wrap features a slightly different kind of cable called Twists that are worked with a purl stitch and 3 knit stitches. Just follow the instructions on page 70 for the Twist 4 Front and the Twist 4 Back. Watch these techniques online at www.leisurearts.com/5648.

STITCH GUIDE

TWIST 4 FRONT (*abbreviated* **T4F**)
Slip 3 sts onto cable needle and hold in **front** of work, P1 from left needle, K3 from cable needle.

TWIST 4 BACK (*abbreviated* **T4B**)
Slip st onto cable needle and hold in **back** of work, K3 from left needle, P1 from cable needle.

CABLE 6 FRONT
 (*abbreviated* **C6F**)
Slip 3 sts onto cable needle and hold in **front** of work, K3 from left needle, K3 from cable needle.

CABLE 6 BACK (*abbreviated* **C6B**)
Slip 3 sts onto cable needle and hold in **back** of work, K3 from left needle, K3 from cable needle.

CENTER CABLE (uses 44 sts)
Row 1: P 19, K6, P 19.
Row 2: K 19, P6, K 19.
Rows 3 and 4: Repeat Rows 1 and 2.
Row 5: P 19, C6B, P 19.
Row 6: K 19, P6, K 19.
Row 7: P 18, T4B, T4F, P 18.
Row 8: K 18, P3, K2, P3, K 18.
Row 9: P 17, T4B, P2, T4F, P 17.
Row 10: K 17, P3, K4, P3, K 17.
Row 11: P 16, T4B, P4, T4F, P 16.

Row 12: K 16, P3, K6, P3, K 16.
Row 13: P 15, T4B, P6, T4F, P 15.
Row 14: K 15, P3, K8, P3, K 15.
Row 15: P 14, T4B, P8, T4F, P 14.
Row 16: K 14, P3, K 10, P3, K 14.
Row 17: P 13, T4B, P 10, T4F, P 13.
Row 18: K 13, P3, K 12, P3, K 13.
Row 19: P 12, T4B, P 12, T4F, P 12.
Row 20: K 12, P3, K 14, P3, K 12.
Row 21: P 11, T4B, P 14, T4F, P 11.
Row 22: K 11, P3, K 16, P3, K 11.
Row 23: P 11, T4F, P 14, T4B, P 11.
Row 24: K 12, P3, K 14, P3, K 12.
Row 25: P 12, T4F, P 12, T4B, P 12.
Row 26: K 13, P3, K 12, P3, K 13.
Row 27: P 13, T4F, P 10, T4B, P 13.
Row 28: K 14, P3, K 10, P3, K 14.
Row 29: P 14, T4F, P8, T4B, P 14.
Row 30: K 15, P3, K8, P3, K 15.
Row 31: P 15, T4F, P6, T4B, P 15.
Row 32: K 16, P3, K6, P3, K 16.
Row 33: P 16, T4F, P4, T4B, P 16.
Row 34: K 17, P3, K4, P3, K 17.
Row 35: P 17, T4F, P2, T4B, P 17.
Row 36: K 18, P3, K2, P3, K 18.
Row 37: P 18, T4F, T4B, P 18.
Row 38: K 19, P6, K 19.
Row 39: P 19, C6B, P 19.
Row 40: K 19, P6, K 19.
Repeat Rows 1-40 for pattern.

CENTER CABLE CHART

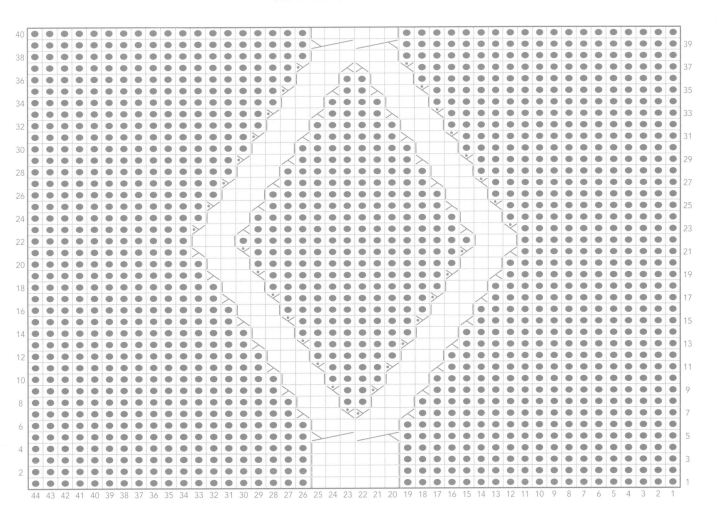

CABLE 6 FRONT

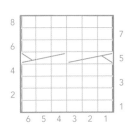

CABLE 6 BACK

KEY

☐ Knit on **right** side, purl on **wrong** side

⦿ Purl on **right** side, knit on **wrong** side

⬚ C6B

⬚ C6F

⬚ T4B

⬚ T4F

On **right** side rows, follow Chart from **right** to **left**;

on **wrong** side rows, follow Chart from **left** to **right**.

INSTRUCTIONS

BORDER

On **wrong** side rows, slip first st as if to **knit**; on **right** side rows, slip first st as if to **purl**.

Cast on 82 sts.

Row 1: Slip 1, P1, (K1, P1) across.

Row 2: Slip 1, K1, (P1, K1) across.

Rows 3-7: Repeat Rows 1 and 2 twice, then repeat Row 1 once **more**.

FIRST END

Row 1 (Buttonhole row): Slip 1, K1, P1, K1, [YO, P2 tog **(buttonhole made)]**, P7, K6, work Row 1 of Center Cable, K6, P6, K1, (P1, K1) 3 times.

Row 2: Slip 1, P1, (K1, P1) twice, K7, P6, work next row of Center Cable, P6, K6, P1, (K1, P1) 3 times.

Row 3: Slip 1, K1, (P1, K1) twice, P7, K6, work next row of Center Cable, K6, P6, K1, (P1, K1) 3 times.

Row 4: Repeat Row 2.

Row 5: Slip 1, K1, (P1, K1) twice, P7, C6B, work next row of Center Cable, C6F, P6, K1, (P1, K1) 3 times.

Rows 6-12: Repeat Rows 2 and 3, 3 times, then repeat Row 2 once **more**.

Rows 13-24: Repeat Rows 5-12 once; then repeat Rows 5-8 once **more**.

Row 25 (Buttonhole row): Slip 1, K1, P1, K1, [YO, P2 tog **(buttonhole made)]**, P7, K6, work next row of Center Cable, K6, P6, K1, (P1, K1) 3 times.

Repeat Rows 2-25, 3 times **more**: 5 buttonholes completed.

CENTER

Beginning with Row 10, repeat Rows 5-12 of First End for pattern, ending by working Row 26 of the 6th repeat of the Center Cable.

SECOND END

Row 1 (Buttonhole row)**:** Slip 1, K1, P1, K1, **[YO, P2 tog (buttonhole made)]**, P7, K6, work next row of Center Cable, K6, P6, K1, (P1, K1) 3 times.

Repeat Rows 2-25 of First End, 4 times: 5 buttonholes completed.

BORDER

Row 1: Slip 1, P1, (K1, P1) across.

Row 2: Slip 1, K1,(P1, K1) across.

Rows 3-7: Repeat Rows 1 and 2 twice, then repeat Row 1 once **more**.

Bind off all sts in **knit**.

Sew buttons opposite buttonholes.

Sweater

No wardrobe is complete without a classic cable sweater! This design is loaded with elegant features, from the generous ribbed neckband to the petite cable braids down the front and sleeves. The drop-shoulder shaping ensures that this sweater will become a comfortable favorite.

Sweater

■■■□ INTERMEDIATE

SIZE INFORMATION

Size	Finished Chest Measurement
X-Small	34½" (87.5 cm)
Small	38" (96.5 cm)
Medium	42" (106.5 cm)
Large	46¼" (117.5 cm)
X-Large	50½" (128.5 cm)
2X-Large	54¾" (139 cm)

Size **Note:** We have printed the instructions in different colors to make it easier for you to find:

• **Size X-Small in Purple**
• **Size Small in Blue**
• **Size Medium in Pink**
• Size Large in Lime
• **Size X-Large in Dark Blue**
• **Size 2X-Large in Green**

Instructions in Black apply to all sizes.

SHOPPING LIST

Yarn (Medium Weight) **4 MEDIUM**
[3.5 ounces, 197 yards
(100 grams, 180 meters) per hank]:
☐ {6-7-8}{9-9-10} hanks

Knitting Needles
Straight,
☐ Size 6 (4 mm) **or** size needed for gauge

Additional Supplies
☐ Cable needle
☐ Markers
☐ Stitch holders - 2
☐ Yarn needle

GAUGE INFORMATION

In Stockinette Stitch
   (knit one row, purl one row),
   19 sts and 29 rows = 4" (10 cm)

TECHNIQUES USED

• M1 (**Figs. 22a & b, page 88**)
• K2 tog (**Fig. 25, page 89**)
• SSK (**Figs. 26a-c, page 89**)
• P2 tog tbl (**Fig. 28, page 90**)
• SSP (**Fig. 29, page 90**)

STITCH GUIDE

CABLE 4 FRONT (*abbreviated* **C4F**)

Slip 2 sts onto cable needle and hold in **front** of work, K2 from left needle, K2 from cable needle.

CABLE 4 BACK (*abbreviated* **C4B**)

Slip 2 sts onto cable needle and hold in **back** of work, K2 from left needle, K2 from cable needle.

FRONT CABLE (uses 32 sts)

Row 1 (Right side)**:** P2, K8, P2, C4F, C4B, P2, K8, P2.

Row 2: (K2, P8) 3 times, K2.

Row 3: P2, C4B, C4F, P2, K8, P2, C4B, C4F, P2.

Row 4: (K2, P8) 3 times, K2.

Repeat Rows 1-4 for pattern.

SLEEVE CABLE (uses 12 sts)

Row 1 (Right side)**:** P2, C4F, C4B, P2.

Row 2: K2, P8, K2.

Row 3: P2, K8, P2.

Row 4: K2, P8, K2.

Repeat Rows 1-4 for pattern.

FRONT CHART

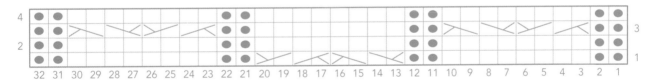

KEY

☐ Knit on **right** side, purl on **wrong** side

⦿ Purl on **right** side, knit on **wrong** side

C4B

C4F

On **right** side rows, follow Chart from **right** to **left**;
on **wrong** side rows, follow Chart from **left** to **right**.

INSTRUCTIONS
Back
RIBBING

Cast on {84-92-102}
{112-122-132} sts.

Row 1: K{1-1-0}{1-0-1}
(*see Zeros, page 87*), P2,
(K2, P2) across to last
{1-1-0}{1-0-1} st,
K{1-1-0}{1-0-1}.

Row 2: P{1-1-0}{1-0-1},
K2, (P2, K2) across to
last {1-1-0}{1-0-1} st,
P{1-1-0}{1-0-1}.

Repeat Rows 1 and 2
until Ribbing measures
approximately 3" (7.5 cm)
from cast on edge, ending
by working Row 2.

BODY

Beginning with a **knit** row,
 work in Stockinette Stitch until
piece measures approximately
15" (38 cm) from cast on edge.

ARMHOLE SHAPING

Rows 1 and 2: Bind off {5-7-10}
{13-16-18} sts, work across:
{74-78-82}{86-90-96} sts.

Work even until Armholes
measure approximately
{7-7½-8}{8½-9-9}"/{18-19-20.5}
{21.5-23-23} cm, ending by
working a **knit** row.

SHOULDER SHAPING

Rows 1-4: Bind off {8-8-9}
{9-9-10} sts, work across:
{42-46-46}{50-54-56} sts.

Rows 5 and 6: Bind off {9-10-9}
{10-11-11} sts, work across:
{24-26-28}{30-32-34} sts.

Slip remaining sts onto st
holder.

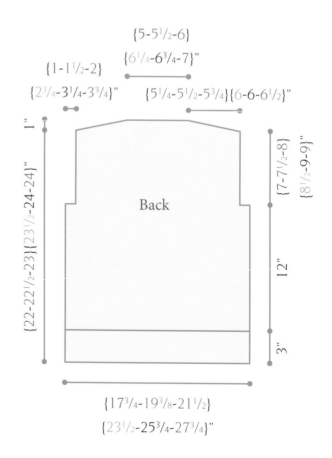

{5-5½-6}
{6¼-6¾-7}"

{1-1½-2}
{2¾-3¼-3¾}"

{5¼-5½-5¾}{6-6-6½}"

1"

{22-22½-23}{23½-24-24}"

{7-7½-8}
{8½-9-9}"

Back

12"

3"

{17¾-19⅜-21½}
{23½-25¾-27¾}"

Front
RIBBING

Cast on {84-92-102} {112-122-132} sts.

Row 1: K{1-1-0}{1-0-1}, P2, (K2, P2) across to last {1-1-0} {1-0-1} st, K{1-1-0}{1-0-1}.

Row 2: P{1-1-0}{1-0-1}, K2, (P2, K2) across to last {1-1-0} {1-0-1} st, P{1-1-0}{1-0-1}.

Repeat Rows 1 and 2 until Ribbing measures approximately 3" (7.5 cm) from cast on edge, ending by working Row 1.

Increase Row: Work in ribbing pattern across {33-37-42} {47-52-57} sts, M1, (work 2 sts, M1) 9 times, work across: {94-102-112}{122-132-142} sts.

BODY

Row 1: K{31-35-40}{45-50-55}, place marker (**see Markers, page 87**), work Row 1 of Front Cable, place marker, knit across.

Row 2: Purl across to next marker, work next row of Front Cable, purl across.

Row 3: Knit across to next marker, work next row of Front Cable, knit across.

Repeat Rows 2 and 3 for pattern until piece measures approximately 15" (38 cm) from cast on edge.

ARMHOLE SHAPING

Maintain established pattern throughout.

Rows 1 and 2: Bind off {5-7-10} {13-16-18} sts, work across: {84-88-92}{96-100-106} sts.

Work even until Armholes measure approximately {6-6½-7}{7½-8-8}"/{15-16.5-18} {19-20.5-20.5} cm, ending by working a **knit** row.

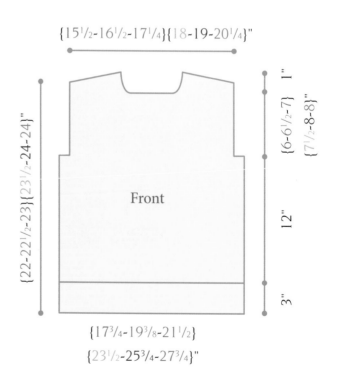

{15½-16½-17¼}{18-19-20¼}"

{22-22½-23}{23½-24-24}"

Front

{6-6½-7}
{7½-8-8}"

1"

12"

3"

{17¾-19⅜-21½}
{23½-25¾-27¾}"

NECK SHAPING

Both sides of the Neck are worked at the same time, using separate hanks of yarn.

Row 1: Purl across to first marker, slip next 32 sts onto second st holder; with second yarn, purl across: {26-28-30}{32-34-37} sts **each** side.

Row 2 (Decrease row): Knit across to within 2 sts of neck edge, K2 tog; with second yarn, SSK, knit across: {25-27-29}{31-33-36} sts **each** side.

Sizes Small, Medium, Large, X-Large, & 2X-Large ONLY
Row 3 (Decrease row): Purl across to within 2 sts of neck edge, P2 tog tbl; with second yarn, SSP, purl across: {26-28}{30-32-35} sts **each** side.

Size Medium ONLY
Row 4: Repeat Row 2: 27 sts **each** side.

Sizes Large, X-Large, & 2X-Large ONLY
Rows 4 thru {5-6-7}: Repeat Rows 2 and 3, {1-1-2} time(s); then repeat Row 2, {0-1-0} time(s) **more**: {28-29-31} sts **each** side.

All Sizes
Work even for {5-4-3}{2-1-0} row(s).

SHOULDER SHAPING
Rows 1-4: Bind off {8-8-9}{9-9-10} sts, work across; with second yarn, work across: {9-10-9}{10-11-11} sts **each** side.

Row 5: Bind off {9-10-9}{10-11-11} sts; with second yarn, work across.

Bind off remaining {9-10-9}{10-11-11} sts.

Sleeve (Make 2)
RIBBING

Cast on {34-36-38}{40-42-44} sts.

Row 1: K{0-1-0}{1-0-1}, P2, (K2, P2) across to last {0-1-0}{1-0-1} st, K{0-1-0}{1-0-1}.

Row 2: P{0-1-0}{1-0-1}, K2, (P2, K2) across to last {0-1-0} {1-0-1} st, P{0-1-0}{1-0-1}.

Repeat Rows 1 and 2 until Ribbing measures approximately 3" (7.5 cm) from cast on edge, ending by working Row 1.

Sizes X-Small, Small, & Medium ONLY

Increase Row: P{15-16-17}, M1, (P1, M1) 3 times, purl across: {38-40-42} sts.

Size Large ONLY

Increase Row: (P9, M1) twice, (P1, M1) 3 times, P 10, M1, P9: 46 sts.

Size X-Large ONLY

Increase Row: (P5, M1) 3 times, P4, M1, (P1, M1) 3 times, P5, (M1, P5) 3 times: 52 sts.

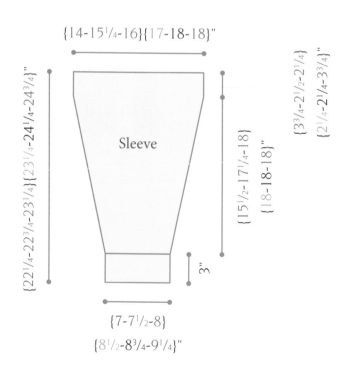

{14-15¼-16}{17-18-18}"

{22¼-22¾-23¼}{23¼-24¼-24¾}"

{15½-17¼-18}{18-18-18}"

{3¾-2½-2¼}{2¼-2¼-3¾}"

Sleeve

3"

{7-7½-8}
{8½-8¾-9¼}"

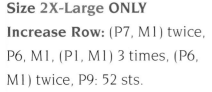

Size 2X-Large ONLY
Increase Row: (P7, M1) twice, P6, M1, (P1, M1) 3 times, (P6, M1) twice, P9: 52 sts.

BODY
Row 1: K{13-14-15}{17-20-20}, place marker, work Row 1 of Sleeve Cable, place marker, knit across.

Row 2: Purl across to next marker, work next row of Sleeve Cable, purl across.

Row 3: Knit across to next marker, work next row of Sleeve Cable, knit across.

Rows 4-6: Repeat Rows 2 and 3 once, then repeat Row 2 once **more**.

Row 7 (Increase row)**:** K1, M1, knit across to next marker, work next row of Sleeve Cable, knit across to last st, M1, K1: {40-42-44}{48-54-54} sts.

Rows 8-12: Work even in established pattern.

Continue to increase 1 st at **each** side in same manner, every sixth row, {2-9-10}{10-10-10} times, then increase every eighth row, {13-8-8}{8-8-8} times: {70-76-80}{84-90-90} sts.

Work even until Sleeve measures approximately {22¼-22¾-23¼}{23¾-24¼-24¾}"/ {56.5-58-59}{60.5-61.5-63} cm from cast on edge.

Bind off all sts.

SLEEVE CHART

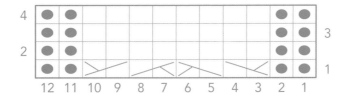

KEY

☐ Knit on **right** side, purl on **wrong** side

⬤ Purl on **right** side, knit on **wrong** side

⟍⟋ C4B

⟋⟍ C4F

On **right** side rows, follow Chart from **right** to **left**;
on **wrong** side rows, follow Chart from **left** to **right**.

FINISHING

Sew right shoulder seam.

NECKBAND

With **right** side facing, pick up {11-11-11}{12-12-12} sts along left Front Neck Shaping (**Figs. 30a & b, page 91**), K 32 from Front st holder, pick up {11-11-11}{12-12-12} sts along right Front Neck Shaping, K{24-26-28}{30-32-34} sts from Back st holder: {78-80-82}{86-88-90} sts.

Row 1: P{0-1-0}{0-1-0}, K2, (P2, K2) across to last {0-1-0} {0-1-0} st, P{0-1-0}{0-1-0}.

Row 2: K{0-1-0}{0-1-0}, P2, (K2, P2) across to last {{0-1-0} {0-1-0} st, K{0-1-0}{0-1-0}.

Repeat Rows 1 and 2 until Neckband measures approximately 2¹⁄₂" (6.5 cm).

Bind off **loosely** in pattern.

Sew left shoulder seam.

Matching center of last row to shoulder seam, sew top of each Sleeve along Armhole edge and sides of Sleeve to bound off edges (**Fig. A**).

Fig. A

shoulder seam

X   X

X   X

center

Weave underarm and side in one continuous seam (**Fig. 31, page 91**).

General Instructions

ABBREVIATIONS

C4B	Cable 4 Back
C4F	Cable 4 Front
C6B	Cable 6 Back
C6F	Cable 6 Front
C8B	Cable 8 Back
C8F	Cable 8 Front
C12B	Cable 12 Back
C12F	Cable 12 Front
cm	centimeters
K	knit
LT	Left Twist
M1	make one
mm	millimeters
P	purl
Rnd(s)	Round(s)
SSK	slip, slip, knit
SSP	slip, slip, purl
st(s)	stitch(es)
T4B	Twist 4 Back
T4F	Twist 4 Front
tbl	through back loop(s)
tog	together
YO	yarn over

SYMBOLS & TERMS

★ — work instructions following ★ as **many more** times as indicated in addition to the first time.

( ) or [ ] — work enclosed instructions **as many** times as specified by the number immediately following **or** contains explanatory remarks.

colon (:) — the number(s) given after a colon at the end of a row or round denote(s) the number of stitches you should have on that row or round.

work even — work without increasing or decreasing in the established pattern.

KNIT TERMINOLOGY	
UNITED STATES	**INTERNATIONAL**
gauge =	tension
bind off =	cast off
yarn over (YO) =	yarn forward (yfwd) **or** yarn around needle (yrn)

Yarn Weight Symbol & Names	LACE **0**	SUPER FINE **1**	FINE **2**	LIGHT **3**	MEDIUM **4**	BULKY **5**	SUPER BULKY **6**
Type of Yarns in Category	Fingering, size 10 crochet thread	Sock, Fingering, Baby	Sport, Baby	DK, Light Worsted	Worsted, Afghan, Aran	Chunky, Craft, Rug	Bulky, Roving
Knit Gauge Range* in Stockinette St to 4" (10 cm)	33-40** sts	27-32 sts	23-26 sts	21-24 sts	16-20 sts	12-15 sts	6-11 sts
Advised Needle Size Range	000-1	1 to 3	3 to 5	5 to 7	7 to 9	9 to 11	11 and larger

*GUIDELINES ONLY: The chart above reflects the most commonly used gauges and needle sizes for specific yarn categories.

** Lace weight yarns are usually knitted on larger needles to create lacy openwork patterns. Accordingly, a gauge range is difficult to determine. Always follow the gauge stated in your pattern.

GAUGE

Exact gauge is **essential** for proper size. Before beginning your project, make a sample swatch in the yarn and needle specified. After completing the swatch, measure it, counting your stitches and rows carefully. If your swatch is larger or smaller than specified, **make another, changing needle size to get the correct gauge**. Keep trying until you find the size needles that will give you the specified gauge. Once proper gauge is obtained, measure width of project approximately every 3" (7.5 cm) to be sure gauge remains consistent.

MARKERS

As a convenience to you, we have used markers to help distinguish the beginning of a pattern or the beginning of a round. Place markers as instructed. You may use purchased markers or tie a length of contrasting color yarn around the needle. When you reach a marker on each row or round, slip it from the left needle to the right needle; remove it when no longer needed.

ZEROS

To consolidate the length of an involved pattern, zeros are sometimes used so that all sizes can be combined. For example, decrease every sixth row, {5-1-0} time(s) means the first size would decrease 5 times, the second size would decrease once, and the third size would do nothing.

KNITTING NEEDLES		
UNITED STATES	ENGLISH U.K.	METRIC (mm)
0	13	2
1	12	2.25
2	11	2.75
3	10	3.25
4	9	3.5
5	8	3.75
6	7	4
7	6	4.5
8	5	5
9	4	5.5
10	3	6
10½	2	6.5
11	1	8
13	00	9
15	000	10
17	---	12.75
19	---	15
35	---	19
50	---	25

BEGINNER	Projects for first-time knitters using basic knit and purl stitches. Minimal shaping.
EASY	Projects using basic stitches, repetitive stitch patterns, simple color changes, and simple shaping and finishing.
INTERMEDIATE	Projects with a variety of stitches, such as basic cables and lace, simple intarsia, double-pointed needles and knitting in the round needle techniques, mid-level shaping and finishing.
EXPERIENCED	Projects using advanced techniques and stitches, such as short rows, fair isle, more intricate intarsia, cables, lace patterns, and numerous color changes.

MAKE ONE (abbreviated M1)

Insert the **left** needle under the horizontal strand between the stitches from the front (**Fig. 22a**). Then knit into the **back** of the strand (**Fig. 22b**).

Fig. 22a

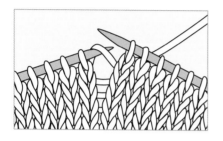

Fig. 22b

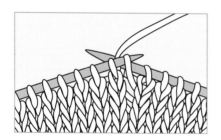

ADDING NEW STITCHES

Insert the right needle into stitch as if to **knit**, yarn over and pull loop through (**Fig. 23a**), insert the left needle into the loop just worked from **front** to **back** and slip the loop onto the left needle (**Fig. 23b**). Repeat for required number of stitches.

Fig. 23a

Fig. 23b

YARN OVER

Bring yarn forward **between** the needles, then back **over** the top of the right hand needle and forward **between** the needles again, so that it is now in position to purl the next stitch (**Fig. 24**).

Fig. 24

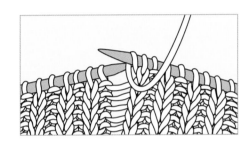

KNIT 2 TOGETHER

(*abbreviated K2 tog*)

Insert the right needle into the **front** of the first two stitches on the left needle as if to **knit** (**Fig. 25**), then **knit** them together as if they were one stitch.

Fig. 25

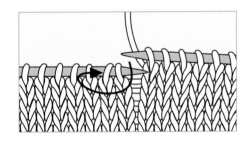

SLIP, SLIP, KNIT

(*abbreviated SSK*)

Separately slip two stitches as if to **knit** (**Fig. 26a**). Insert the left needle into the **front** of both slipped stitches (**Fig. 26b**) and knit them together (**Fig. 26c**).

Fig. 26a

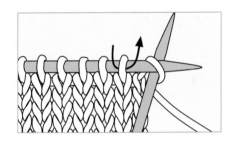

Fig. 26b

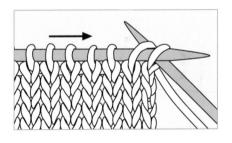

Fig. 26c

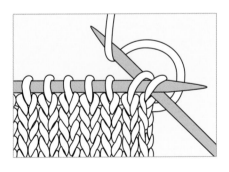

PURL 2 TOGETHER

(*abbreviated P2 tog*)

Insert the right needle into the **front** of the first two stitches on the left needle as if to **purl** (**Fig. 27**), then **purl** them together.

Fig. 27

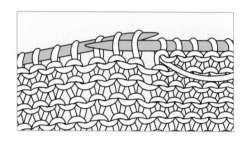

PURL 2 TOGETHER THROUGH THE BACK LOOP

(*abbreviated P2 tog tbl*)

Insert the right needle into the **back** of both stitches from **back** to **front** (**Fig. 28**), then **purl** them together.

Fig. 28

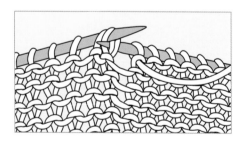

SLIP, SLIP, PURL

(*abbreviated SSP*)

Separately slip two stitches as if to **knit**. Place these two stitches **back** onto the left needle. Insert the right needle into the **back** of both stitches from **back** to **front** (**Fig. 29**) and purl them together.

Fig. 29

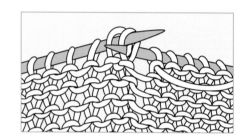

PICKING UP STITCHES

When instructed to pick up stitches, insert the needle from the **front** to the **back** under two strands at the edge of the worked piece. Put the yarn around the needle as if to **knit** (**Figs. 30a & b**), then bring the needle with the yarn back through the stitch to the right side, resulting in a stitch on the needle. Repeat this along the edge, picking up the required number of stitches.

A crochet hook may be helpful to pull yarn through.

Fig. 30a

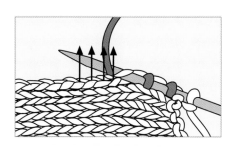

Fig. 30b

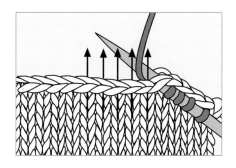

WEAVING SEAMS

With the **right** side of both pieces facing you and edges even, sew through both sides once to secure the seam. Insert the needle under the bar **between** the first and second stitches on the row and pull the yarn through (**Fig. 31**). Insert the needle under the next bar on the second side. Repeat from side to side, being careful to match rows. If the edges are different lengths, it may be necessary to insert the needle under two bars at one edge.

Fig. 31

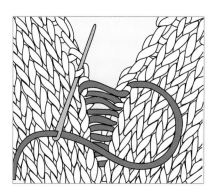

Knit Basics

KNIT STITCH (*abbreviated* **K**)
ENGLISH METHOD

Step 1: Hold the needle with the stitches in your left hand and the empty needle in your right hand.

Step 2: With the working yarn in **back** of the needles, insert the right needle into the stitch closest to the tip of the left needle as shown in *Fig. 32a*.

Fig. 32a

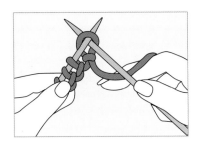

Step 3: Hold the right needle with your left thumb and index finger while you bring the yarn beneath the right needle and between the needles from **back** to **front** (*Fig. 32b*).

Fig. 32b

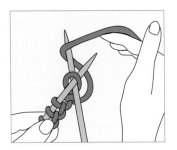

Step 4: With your right hand, bring the right needle (with the loop of yarn) toward you and through the stitch (*Figs. 32c & d*), slip the old stitch off the left needle and gently pull to tighten the new stitch on the shaft of the right needle.

Fig. 32c   Fig. 32d

 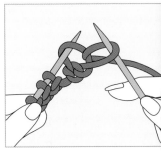

CONTINENTAL METHOD

Step 1: Hold the needle with the stitches in your left hand and the empty needle in your right hand. Loop the working yarn over the index finger of you left hand and hold it loosely across the palm of your hand with your little finger.

Step 2: With the yarn in **back** of the needles, insert the right needle into the stitch closest to the tip of the left needle as shown in *Fig. 33a*.

Fig. 33a

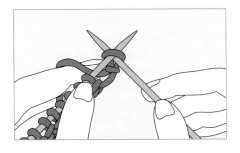

Step 3: With your left index finger, bring the yarn between the needles from **left** to **right** (Fig. 33b).

Fig. 33b

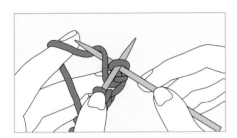

Step 4: With your **right** hand, bring the right needle (with the loop of yarn) toward you and through the stitch (Figs. 33c & d), slip the old stitch off the left needle and gently pull to tighten the new stitch on the shaft of the right needle.

Fig. 33c

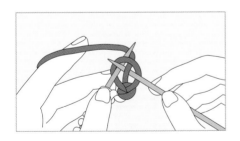

Fig. 33d

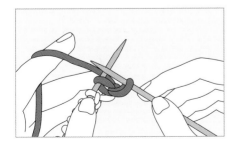

PURL STITCH (*abbreviated* P)
ENGLISH METHOD

Step 1: Hold the needle with the stitches in your left hand and the empty needle in your right hand.

Step 2: With the yarn in **front** of the needles, insert the right needle into the front of the stitch as shown in Fig. 34a.

Fig. 34a

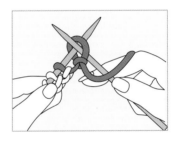

Step 3: Hold the right needle with your left thumb and index finger while you bring the yarn between the needles from **right** to **left** and around the right needle (Fig. 34b).

Fig. 34b

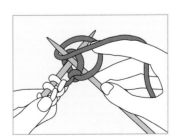

Step 4: Move the right needle (with the loop of yarn) through the stitch and away from you (**Fig. 34c**), slip the old stitch off the left needle and gently pull to tighten the new stitch on the shaft of the right needle.

Fig. 34c

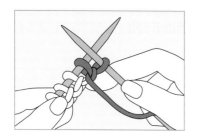

CONTINENTAL METHOD

Step 1: Hold the needle with the stitches in your left hand and the empty needle in your right hand. Loop the working yarn over the index finger of your left hand and hold it loosely across the palm of your hand with your little finger.

Step 2: With the yarn in **front** of the needles, insert the right needle into the front of the stitch as shown in **Fig. 35a.**

Fig. 35a

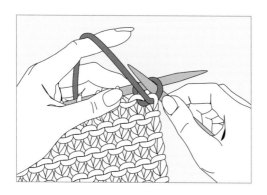

Step 3: With your index finger, bring the yarn between the needles from **right** to **left** around the right needle (**Fig. 35b**).

Fig. 35b

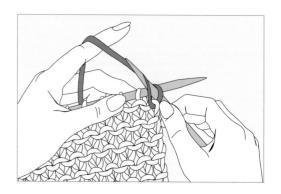

Step 4: Move your left index finger forward while moving the right needle (with the loop of yarn) through the stitch and away from you (**Fig. 35c**), slip the old stitch off the left needle and gently pull to tighten the new stitch on the shaft of the right needle.

Fig. 35c

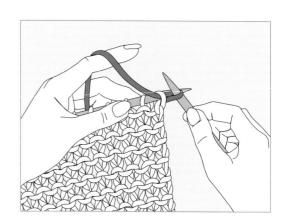

BIND OFF

Binding off is the method used to remove and secure your stitches from the knitting needles so that they don't unravel. Work the first two stitches. Use your left needle as a tool to lift the second stitch on the right needle up and over the first stitch (**Fig. 36a**) and completely off the right needle (**Fig. 36b**). Don't forget to remove the left needle from the stitch.

Fig. 36a

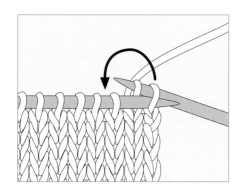

Fig. 36b

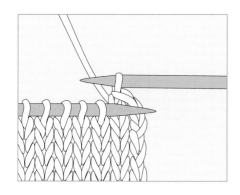

You now have one stitch on your right needle and you have bound off one stitch. Count the stitch as you bind it off, not as you work it.

Work the next stitch; you will have two stitches on your right needle. Bind off as before.

Continue until your left needle is empty and there is only one stitch left on your right needle.

Cut the yarn, leaving a long end to hide later.

Slip the stitch off the right needle, pull the end through the stitch (**Fig. 36c**) and tighten the stitch.

Fig. 36c

Yarn Information

Projects in this book were made using various weights of yarn. Any brand of the specified weight of yarn may be used. It is best to refer to the yardage/meters when determining how many balls or skeins to purchase. Remember, to arrive at the finished size, it is the GAUGE/TENSION that is important, not the brand of yarn. For your convenience, listed below are the specific yarns used to create our photography models.

BELT
Rowan® Wool Cotton

#965 Mocha

FINGERLESS GLOVES
Rowan® Pure Wool DK

#046 Tudor Rose

VEST
Berroco® Flicker®

#3312 Odile

SCARF
Lion Brand® Wool-Ease®

#188 Paprika

CAR SEAT COVER
Bernat® Softee® Baby™

#30201 Aqua

WRAP
Classic Elite Kumara

#5792 Royce Mountain

FELTED CLUTCH
Patons® Classic Wool

#00240 Leaf Green

CUSHION
Patons® Classic Wool Roving

#77010 Natural

SWEATER
Berroco® Lustra®

#3162 Ratatouille

HAT
Berroco® Ultra® Alpaca Light

#4213 Blue Glasynys

Your

PLEASE SHARE
your comments and suggestions at
www.facebook.com/Official.LeisureArts

PLUS you can find us on Twitter,
Pinterest, and YouTube!!

opinion matters!